VIOLIN

101 MOVIE HITS

Available for
FLUTE, CLARINET, ALTO SAX, TENOR SAX, TRUMPET,
HORN, TROMBONE, VIOLIN, VIOLA, CELLO

ISBN 978-1-4950-6070-0

HAL•LEONARD®
CORPORATION
7777 W. BLUEMOUND RD. P.O. BOX 13819 MILWAUKEE, WI 53213

Visit Hal Leonard Online at
www.halleonard.com

CONTENTS

AGAINST ALL ODDS
(Take a Look at Me Now)
from AGAINST ALL ODDS

Violin

Words and Music by
PHIL COLLINS

ALFIE
Theme from the Paramount Picture ALFIE

VIOLIN

Words by HAL DAVID
Music by BURT BACHARACH

AXEL F
Theme from the Paramount Motion Picture BEVERLY HILLS COP

VIOLIN

By HAROLD FALTERMEYER

BABY ELEPHANT WALK

from the Paramount Picture HATARI!

VIOLIN

By HENRY MANCINI

BEAUTY AND THE BEAST

from Walt Disney's BEAUTY AND THE BEAST

VIOLIN

Music by ALAN MENKEN
Lyrics by HOWARD ASHMAN

BLAZE OF GLORY
featured in the film YOUNG GUNS II

VIOLIN

Words and Music by
JON BON JOVI

BLUE VELVET

featured in the Motion Picture BLUE VELVET

VIOLIN

Words and Music by BERNIE WAYNE
and LEE MORRIS

BORN FREE
from the Columbia Pictures' Release BORN FREE

VIOLIN

Words by DON BLACK
Music by JOHN BARRY

CALL ME
from the Paramount Motion Picture AMERICAN GIGOLO

VIOLIN

Words by DEBORAH HARRY
Music by GIORGIO MORODER

Moderately fast

CAN YOU FEEL THE LOVE TONIGHT
from Walt Disney Pictures' THE LION KING

VIOLIN

Music by ELTON JOHN
Lyrics by TIM RICE

Pop Ballad

CAN'T HELP FALLING IN LOVE

from the Paramount Picture BLUE HAWAII

VIOLIN

Words and Music by GEORGE DAVID WEISS,
HUGO PERETTI and LUIGI CREATORE

THE CANDY MAN

from WILLY WONKA AND THE CHOCOLATE FACTORY

Violin

Words and Music by LESLIE BRICUSSE
and ANTHONY NEWLEY

CHARIOTS OF FIRE
from CHARIOTS OF FIRE

VIOLIN

By VANGELIS

COLORS OF THE WIND
from Walt Disney's POCAHONTAS

VIOLIN

Music by ALAN MENKEN
Lyrics by STEPHEN SCHWARTZ

D.S. al Coda

CODA

COME SATURDAY MORNING
(Saturday Morning)
from the Paramount Picture THE STERILE CUCKOO

VIOLIN

Words by DORY PREVIN
Music by FRED KARLIN

CUPS
(When I'm Gone)

from the Motion Picture Soundtrack PITCH PERFECT

VIOLIN

Words and Music by A.P. CARTER,
LUISA GERSTEIN and HELOISE TUNSTALL-BEHRENS

COME WHAT MAY

from the Motion Picture MOULIN ROUGE

VIOLIN

Words and Music by
DAVID BAERWALD

Slowly

DANGER ZONE
from the Motion Picture TOP GUN

VIOLIN

Words and Music by GIORGIO MORODER
and TOM WHITLOCK

DEAR HEART
from DEAR HEART

Violin

Music by HENRY MANCINI
Words by JAY LIVINGSTON and RAY EVANS

Moderately

DIAMONDS ARE A GIRL'S BEST FRIEND

from GENTLEMEN PREFER BLONDES

VIOLIN

Words by LEO ROBIN
Music by JULE STYNE

Moderately fast

DO YOU KNOW WHERE YOU'RE GOING TO?

Theme from MAHOGANY

Violin

Words by GERRY GOFFIN
Music by MICHAEL MASSER

DON'T YOU (FORGET ABOUT ME)

from the Universal Picture THE BREAKFAST CLUB

VIOLIN

Words and Music by KEITH FORSEY
and STEVE SCHIFF

THE DREAME
from the film SENSE AND SENSIBILITY

VIOLIN

By PATRICK DOYLE

END OF THE ROAD
from the Paramount Motion Picture BOOMERANG

VIOLIN

Words and Music by BABYFACE,
L.A. REID and DARYL SIMMONS

ENDLESS LOVE

from ENDLESS LOVE

VIOLIN

Words and Music by
LIONEL RICHIE

EVERYBODY'S TALKIN'

(Echoes)

from MIDNIGHT COWBOY

VIOLIN

Words and Music by
FRED NEIL

EXHALE
(Shoop Shoop)
from WAITING TO EXHALE

VIOLIN

Words and Music by
BABYFACE

EYE OF THE TIGER
Theme from ROCKY III

VIOLIN

Words and Music by FRANK SULLIVAN
and JIM PETERIK

FOOTLOOSE

Theme from the Paramount Motion Picture FOOTLOOSE

VIOLIN

Words by DEAN PITCHFORD
Music by KENNY LOGGINS

FORREST GUMP – MAIN TITLE

(Feather Theme)

from the Paramount Motion Picture FORREST GUMP

VIOLIN

Music by ALAN SILVESTRI

HALLELUJAH

featured in the DreamWorks Motion Picture SHREK

VIOLIN

Words and Music by
LEONARD COHEN

GLORY OF LOVE
Theme from KARATE KID PART II

VIOLIN

Words and Music by DAVID FOSTER,
PETER CETERA and DIANE NINI

Slowly

39

HAPPY

from DESPICABLE ME 2

VIOLIN

Words and Music by
PHARRELL WILLIAMS

THE HEAT IS ON
from the Paramount Motion Picture BEVERLY HILLS COP

VIOLIN

Words by KEITH FORSEY
Music by HAROLD FALTERMEYER

HELLO AGAIN

from the Motion Picture THE JAZZ SINGER

VIOLIN

Words by NEIL DIAMOND
Music by NEIL DIAMOND
and ALAN LINDGREN

HOW DEEP IS YOUR LOVE
from the Motion Picture SATURDAY NIGHT FEVER

Violin

Words and Music by BARRY GIBB,
ROBIN GIBB and MAURICE GIBB

I AM A MAN OF CONSTANT SORROW

featured in O BROTHER, WHERE ART THOU?

VIOLIN

Words and Music by
CARTER STANLEY

Moderately, in 2

I BELIEVE I CAN FLY

from SPACE JAM

VIOLIN

Words and Music by
ROBERT KELLY

I JUST CALLED TO SAY I LOVE YOU

featured in THE WOMAN IN RED

VIOLIN

Words and Music by
STEVIE WONDER

I WILL ALWAYS LOVE YOU
featured in THE BODYGUARD

VIOLIN

Words and Music by
DOLLY PARTON

Moderately slow

small notes optional

I WILL WAIT FOR YOU
from THE UMBRELLAS OF CHERBOURG

VIOLIN

Music by MICHEL LEGRAND
Original French Text by JACQUES DEMY
English Words by NORMAN GIMBEL

(I'VE HAD) THE TIME OF MY LIFE

from DIRTY DANCING

VIOLIN

Words and Music by FRANKE PREVITE,
JOHN DeNICOLA and DONALD MARKOWITZ

JAILHOUSE ROCK

from *JAILHOUSE ROCK*

VIOLIN

Words and Music by JERRY LEIBER
and MIKE STOLLER

THE JOHN DUNBAR THEME

from DANCES WITH WOLVES

Violin

By JOHN BARRY

KOKOMO

from the Motion Picture COCKTAIL

VIOLIN

Words and Music by JOHN PHILLIPS,
TERRY MELCHER, MIKE LOVE,
and SCOTT McKENZIE

Moderately bright

LET THE RIVER RUN
Theme from the Motion Picture WORKING GIRL

VIOLIN

Words and Music by
CARLY SIMON

LET IT GO
from Disney's Animated Feature FROZEN

VIOLIN

Music and Lyrics by KRISTEN ANDERSON-LOPEZ
and ROBERT LOPEZ

Slowly, in 2

LIVE AND LET DIE
from LIVE AND LET DIE

VIOLIN

Words and Music by PAUL McCARTNEY
and LINDA McCARTNEY

THE LOOK OF LOVE

from CASINO ROYALE

VIOLIN

Words by HAL DAVID
Music by BURT BACHARACH

Moderately

LUCK BE A LADY
from GUYS AND DOLLS

Violin

By FRANK LOESSER

A MAN AND A WOMAN
(Un homme et une femme)
from A MAN AND A WOMAN

VIOLIN

Original Words by PIERRE BAROUH
English Words by JERRY KELLER
Music by FRANCIS LAI

MANIAC

from the Paramount Picture FLASHDANCE

VIOLIN

Words and Music by MICHAEL SEMBELLO
and DENNIS MATKOSKY

MISSION: IMPOSSIBLE THEME

from the Paramount Motion Picture MISSION: IMPOSSIBLE

Violin

By LALO SCHIFRIN

MRS. ROBINSON
from THE GRADUATE

VIOLIN

Words and Music by
PAUL SIMON

MOON RIVER

from the Paramount Picture BREAKFAST AT TIFFANY'S

VIOLIN

Words by JOHNNY MERCER
Music by HENRY MANCINI

MORE
(Ti guarderò nel cuore)
from the film MONDO CANE

VIOLIN

Music by NINO OLIVIERO and RIZ ORTOLANI
Italian Lyrics by MARCELLO CIORCIOLINI
English Lyrics by NORMAN NEWELL

Moderately, in 2

THE MUSIC OF GOODBYE

from OUT OF AFRICA

Violin

Words and Music by JOHN BARRY,
ALAN BERGMAN and MARILYN BERGMAN

Moderately

MY HEART WILL GO ON
(Love Theme from 'Titanic')
from the Paramount and Twentieth Century Fox Motion Picture TITANIC

VIOLIN

Music by JAMES HORNER
Lyric by WILL JENNINGS

NINE TO FIVE

from NINE TO FIVE

VIOLIN

Words and Music by
DOLLY PARTON

Moderately, in 2

NOTHING'S GONNA STOP US NOW
featured in MANNEQUIN

VIOLIN

Words and Music by DIANE WARREN
and ALBERT HAMMOND

OLD TIME ROCK & ROLL
featured in RISKY BUSINESS

VIOLIN

Words and Music by GEORGE JACKSON
and THOMAS E. JONES III

Medium Rock

THE PINK PANTHER

from THE PINK PANTHER

Violin

By HENRY MANCINI

PUT YOUR DREAMS AWAY (FOR ANOTHER DAY)

featured in INSIDE MOVES

Violin

Words by RUTH LOWE
Music by STEPHAN WEISS
and PAUL MANN

PUTTIN' ON THE RITZ

from the Motion Picture PUTTIN' ON THE RITZ

VIOLIN

Words and Music by
IRVING BERLIN

QUE SERA, SERA
(Whatever Will Be, Will Be)
from THE MAN WHO KNEW TOO MUCH

VIOLIN

Words and Music by JAY LIVINGSTON
and RAYMOND B. EVANS

THE RAINBOW CONNECTION

from THE MUPPET MOVIE

Violin

Words and Music by PAUL WILLIAMS
and KENNETH L. ASCHER

RAINDROPS KEEP FALLIN' ON MY HEAD

from BUTCH CASSIDY AND THE SUNDANCE KID

VIOLIN

Lyrics by HAL DAVID
Music by BURT BACHARACH

ROCK AROUND THE CLOCK

featured in the Motion Picture BLACKBOARD JUNGLE

Violin

Words and Music by MAX C. FREEDMAN
and JIMMY DeKNIGHT

LOVE THEME FROM "ST. ELMO'S FIRE"

from the Motion Picture ST. ELMO'S FIRE

VIOLIN

Words and Music by
DAVID FOSTER

SAY YOU, SAY ME

from the Motion Picture WHITE NIGHTS

VIOLIN

Words and Music by
LIONEL RICHIE

SEPARATE LIVES
Love Theme from WHITE NIGHTS

VIOLIN

Words and Music by
STEPHEN BISHOP

THE SHADOW OF YOUR SMILE

Love Theme from THE SANDPIPER

Violin

Music by JOHNNY MANDEL
Words by PAUL FRANCIS WEBSTER

SOMEWHERE IN TIME
from SOMEWHERE IN TIME

Violin

By JOHN BARRY

SKYFALL
from the Motion Picture SKYFALL

VIOLIN

Words and Music by ADELE ADKINS
and PAUL EPWORTH

SOMEWHERE, MY LOVE
Lara's Theme from DOCTOR ZHIVAGO

VIOLIN

Lyric by PAUL FRANCIS WEBSTER
Music by MAURICE JARRE

SOMEWHERE OUT THERE

from AN AMERICAN TAIL

Violin

Music by BARRY MANN and JAMES HORNER
Lyrics by CYNTHIA WEIL

Moderately, with expression

THE SOUND OF MUSIC

from THE SOUND OF MUSIC

VIOLIN

Lyrics by OSCAR HAMMERSTEIN II
Music by RICHARD RODGERS

SPEAK SOFTLY, LOVE
(Love Theme)
from the Paramount Picture THE GODFATHER

Words by LARRY KUSIK
Music by NINO ROTA

VIOLIN

STAR TREK® THE MOTION PICTURE

Theme from the Paramount Picture STAR TREK: THE MOTION PICTURE

VIOLIN

Music by
JERRY GOLDSMITH

Moderately fast March

SUMMER NIGHTS

from GREASE

Violin

Lyric and Music by WARREN CASEY
and JIM JACOBS

STAYIN' ALIVE
from the Motion Picture SATURDAY NIGHT FEVER

VIOLIN

Words and Music by BARRY GIBB,
ROBIN GIBB and MAURICE GIBB

THE SWEETHEART TREE

from THE GREAT RACE

VIOLIN

Words by JOHNNY MERCER
Music by HENRY MANCINI

SWINGING ON A STAR

from GOING MY WAY

Violin

Words by JOHNNY BURKE
Music by JIMMY VAN HEUSEN

TAKE MY BREATH AWAY
(Love Theme)
from the Paramount Picture TOP GUN

VIOLIN

Words and Music by GIORGIO MORODER
and TOM WHITLOCK

TAMMY
from TAMMY AND THE BACHELOR

VIOLIN

Words and Music by JAY LIVINGSTON
and RAY EVANS

THANKS FOR THE MEMORY

from the Paramount Picture BIG BROADCAST OF 1938

VIOLIN

Words and Music by LEO ROBIN
and RALPH RAINGER

THAT'S AMORÉ
(That's Love)
from the Paramount Picture THE CADDY

VIOLIN

Words by JACK BROOKS
Music by HARRY WARREN

A TIME FOR US
(Love Theme)
from the Paramount Picture ROMEO AND JULIET

VIOLIN

Words by LARRY KUSIK
and EDDIE SNYDER
Music by NINO ROTA

TIME WARP
from THE ROCKY HORROR PICTURE SHOW

Words and Music by
RICHARD O'BRIEN

VIOLIN

103

TO SIR, WITH LOVE

from TO SIR, WITH LOVE

Words by DON BLACK
Music by MARC LONDON

VIOLIN

UNCHAINED MELODY

from the Motion Picture UNCHAINED

Violin

Lyric by HY ZARET
Music by ALEX NORTH

Moderately slow

Fine

D.C. al Fine

TWO HEARTS
from BUSTER

VIOLIN

Words and Music by PHIL COLLINS
and LAMONT DOZIER

Fast Swing

107

UP WHERE WE BELONG

from the Paramount Picture AN OFFICER AND A GENTLEMAN

VIOLIN

Words by WILL JENNINGS
Music by BUFFY SAINTE-MARIE and JACK NITZSCHE

THE WAY WE WERE

from the Motion Picture THE WAY WE WERE

Violin

Words by ALAN and MARILYN BERGMAN
Music by MARVIN HAMLISCH

WHEN SHE LOVED ME

from Walt Disney Pictures' TOY STORY 2 - A Pixar Film

VIOLIN

Music and Lyrics by
RANDY NEWMAN

WHEN YOU BELIEVE
(From The Prince of Egypt)
from THE PRINCE OF EGYPT

VIOLIN

Words and Music by
STEPHEN SCHWARTZ

WHEN YOU WISH UPON A STAR

from Walt Disney's PINOCCHIO

Violin

Words by NED WASHINGTON
Music by LEIGH HARLINE

Moderately

WHERE DO I BEGIN
(Love Theme)
from the Paramount Picture LOVE STORY

VIOLIN

Words by CARL SIGMAN
Music by FRANCIS LAI

WRITING'S ON THE WALL

from the film SPECTRE

Violin

Words and Music by SAM SMITH
and JAMES NAPIER

YOU LIGHT UP MY LIFE

from YOU LIGHT UP MY LIFE

Words and Music by
JOSEPH BROOKS

VIOLIN

YOU MUST LOVE ME
from the Cinergi Motion Picture EVITA

Violin

Words by TIM RICE
Music by ANDREW LLOYD WEBBER

101 SONGS

BIG COLLECTIONS OF FAVORITE SONGS ARRANGED FOR SOLO INSTRUMENTALISTS.

101 BROADWAY SONGS

00154199	Flute	$15.99
00154200	Clarinet	$15.99
00154201	Alto Sax	$15.99
00154202	Tenor Sax	$16.99
00154203	Trumpet	$15.99
00154204	Horn	$15.99
00154205	Trombone	$15.99
00154206	Violin	$15.99
00154207	Viola	$15.99
00154208	Cello	$15.99

101 DISNEY SONGS

00244104	Flute	$17.99
00244106	Clarinet	$17.99
00244107	Alto Sax	$17.99
00244108	Tenor Sax	$17.99
00244109	Trumpet	$17.99
00244112	Horn	$17.99
00244120	Trombone	$17.99
00244121	Violin	$17.99
00244125	Viola	$17.99
00244126	Cello	$17.99

101 MOVIE HITS

00158087	Flute	$15.9
00158088	Clarinet	$15.9
00158089	Alto Sax	$15.9
00158090	Tenor Sax	$15.99
00158091	Trumpet	$15.9
00158092	Horn	$15.99
00158093	Trombone	$15.99
00158094	Violin	$15.99
00158095	Viola	$15.9
00158096	Cello	$15.9

101 CHRISTMAS SONGS

00278637	Flute	$15.99
00278638	Clarinet	$15.99
00278639	Alto Sax	$15.99
00278640	Tenor Sax	$15.99
00278641	Trumpet	$15.99
00278642	Horn	$14.99
00278643	Trombone	$15.99
00278644	Violin	$15.99
00278645	Viola	$15.99
00278646	Cello	$15.99

101 HIT SONGS

00194561	Flute	$17.99
00197182	Clarinet	$17.99
00197183	Alto Sax	$17.99
00197184	Tenor Sax	$17.99
00197185	Trumpet	$17.99
00197186	Horn	$17.99
00197187	Trombone	$17.99
00197188	Violin	$17.99
00197189	Viola	$17.99
00197190	Cello	$17.99

101 POPULAR SONGS

00224722	Flute	$17.99
00224723	Clarinet	$17.99
00224724	Alto Sax	$17.99
00224725	Tenor Sax	$17.99
00224726	Trumpet	$17.99
00224727	Horn	$17.99
00224728	Trombone	$17.99
00224729	Violin	$17.99
00224730	Viola	$17.99
00224731	Cello	$17.99

101 CLASSICAL THEMES

00155315	Flute	$15.99
00155317	Clarinet	$15.99
00155318	Alto Sax	$15.99
00155319	Tenor Sax	$15.99
00155320	Trumpet	$15.99
00155321	Horn	$15.99
00155322	Trombone	$15.99
00155323	Violin	$15.99
00155324	Viola	$15.99
00155325	Cello	$15.99

101 JAZZ SONGS

00146363	Flute	$15.99
00146364	Clarinet	$15.99
00146366	Alto Sax	$15.99
00146367	Tenor Sax	$15.99
00146368	Trumpet	$15.99
00146369	Horn	$14.99
00146370	Trombone	$15.99
00146371	Violin	$15.99
00146372	Viola	$15.99
00146373	Cello	$15.99

101 MOST BEAUTIFUL SONGS

00291023	Flute	$16.99
00291041	Clarinet	$16.99
00291042	Alto Sax	$17.99
00291043	Tenor Sax	$17.99
00291044	Trumpet	$16.99
00291045	Horn	$16.99
00291046	Trombone	$16.99
00291047	Violin	$16.99
00291048	Viola	$16.99
00291049	Cello	$17.99

See complete song lists and sample pages at www.halleonard.com

HAL•LEONARD®
www.halleonard.com

Prices, contents and availability subject to change without notice.

HAL•LEONARD INSTRUMENTAL PLAY-ALONG

Your favorite songs are arranged just for solo instrumentalists with this outstanding series. Each book includes great full-accompaniment play-along audio so you can sound just like a pro!

Check out **halleonard.com** for songlists and more titles!

12 Pop Hits
12 songs
00261790	Flute	00261795	Horn
00261791	Clarinet	00261796	Trombone
00261792	Alto Sax	00261797	Violin
00261793	Tenor Sax	00261798	Viola
00261794	Trumpet	00261799	Cello

The Very Best of Bach
15 selections
00225371	Flute	00225376	Horn
00225372	Clarinet	00225377	Trombone
00225373	Alto Sax	00225378	Violin
00225374	Tenor Sax	00225379	Viola
00225375	Trumpet	00225380	Cello

The Beatles
15 songs
00225330	Flute	00225335	Horn
00225331	Clarinet	00225336	Trombone
00225332	Alto Sax	00225337	Violin
00225333	Tenor Sax	00225338	Viola
00225334	Trumpet	00225339	Cello

Chart Hits
12 songs
00146207	Flute	00146212	Horn
00146208	Clarinet	00146213	Trombone
00146209	Alto Sax	00146214	Violin
00146210	Tenor Sax	00146211	Trumpet
00146216	Cello		

Christmas Songs
12 songs
00146855	Flute	00146863	Horn
00146858	Clarinet	00146864	Trombone
00146859	Alto Sax	00146866	Violin
00146860	Tenor Sax	00146867	Viola
00146862	Trumpet	00146868	Cello

Contemporary Broadway
15 songs
00298704	Flute	00298709	Horn
00298705	Clarinet	00298710	Trombone
00298706	Alto Sax	00298711	Violin
00298707	Tenor Sax	00298712	Viola
00298708	Trumpet	00298713	Cello

Disney Movie Hits
12 songs
00841420	Flute	00841424	Horn
00841687	Oboe	00841425	Trombone
00841421	Clarinet	00841426	Violin
00841422	Alto Sax	00841427	Viola
00841686	Tenor Sax	00841428	Cello
00841423	Trumpet		

Prices, contents, and availability subject to change without notice.

Disney characters and artwork ™ & © 2021 Disney

Disney Solos
12 songs
00841404	Flute	00841506	Oboe
00841406	Alto Sax	00841409	Trumpet
00841407	Horn	00841410	Violin
00841411	Viola	00841412	Cello
00841405	Clarinet/Tenor Sax		
00841408	Trombone/Baritone		
00841553	Mallet Percussion		

Dixieland Favorites
15 songs
00268756	Flute	0068759	Trumpet
00268757	Clarinet	00268760	Trombone
00268758	Alto Sax		

Billie Eilish
9 songs
00345648	Flute	00345653	Horn
00345649	Clarinet	00345654	Trombone
00345650	Alto Sax	00345655	Violin
00345651	Tenor Sax	00345656	Viola
00345652	Trumpet	00345657	Cello

Favorite Movie Themes
13 songs
00841166	Flute	00841168	Trumpet
00841167	Clarinet	00841170	Trombone
00841169	Alto Sax	00841296	Violin

Gospel Hymns
15 songs
00194648	Flute	00194654	Trombone
00194649	Clarinet	00194655	Violin
00194650	Alto Sax	00194656	Viola
00194651	Tenor Sax	00194657	Cello
00194652	Trumpet		

Great Classical Themes
15 songs
00292727	Flute	00292733	Horn
00292728	Clarinet	00292735	Trombone
00292729	Alto Sax	00292736	Violin
00292730	Tenor Sax	00292737	Viola
00292732	Trumpet	00292738	Cello

The Greatest Showman
8 songs
00277389	Flute	00277394	Horn
00277390	Clarinet	00277395	Trombone
00277391	Alto Sax	00277396	Violin
00277392	Tenor Sax	00277397	Viola
00277393	Trumpet	00277398	Cello

Irish Favorites
31 songs
00842489	Flute	00842495	Trombone
00842490	Clarinet	00842496	Violin
00842491	Alto Sax	00842497	Viola
00842493	Trumpet	00842498	Cello
00842494	Horn		

Michael Jackson
11 songs
00119495	Flute	00119499	Trumpet
00119496	Clarinet	00119501	Trombone
00119497	Alto Sax	00119503	Violin
00119498	Tenor Sax	00119502	Accomp.

Jazz & Blues
14 songs
00841438	Flute	00841441	Trumpet
00841439	Clarinet	00841443	Trombone
00841440	Alto Sax	00841444	Violin
00841442	Tenor Sax		

Jazz Classics
12 songs
00151812	Flute	00151816	Trumpet
00151813	Clarinet	00151818	Trombone
00151814	Alto Sax	00151819	Violin
00151815	Tenor Sax	00151821	Cello

Les Misérables
13 songs
00842292	Flute	00842297	Horn
00842293	Clarinet	00842298	Trombone
00842294	Alto Sax	00842299	Violin
00842295	Tenor Sax	00842300	Viola
00842296	Trumpet	00842301	Cello

Metallica
12 songs
02501327	Flute	02502454	Horn
02501339	Clarinet	02501329	Trombone
02501332	Alto Sax	02501334	Violin
02501333	Tenor Sax	02501335	Viola
02501330	Trumpet	02501338	Cello

Motown Classics
15 songs
00842572	Flute	00842576	Trumpet
00842573	Clarinet	00842578	Trombone
00842574	Alto Sax	00842579	Violin
00842575	Tenor Sax		

Pirates of the Caribbean
16 songs
00842183	Flute	00842188	Horn
00842184	Clarinet	00842189	Trombone
00842185	Alto Sax	00842190	Violin
00842186	Tenor Sax	00842191	Viola
00842187	Trumpet	00842192	Cello

Queen
17 songs
00285402	Flute	00285407	Horn
00285403	Clarinet	00285408	Trombone
00285404	Alto Sax	00285409	Violin
00285405	Tenor Sax	00285410	Viola
00285406	Trumpet	00285411	Cello

Simple Songs
14 songs
00249081	Flute	00249087	Horn
00249093	Oboe	00249089	Trombone
00249082	Clarinet	00249090	Violin
00249083	Alto Sax	00249091	Viola
00249084	Tenor Sax	00249092	Cello
00249086	Trumpet	00249094	Mallets

Superhero Themes
14 songs
00363195	Flute	00363200	Horn
00363196	Clarinet	00363201	Trombone
00363197	Alto Sax	00363202	Violin
00363198	Tenor Sax	00363203	Viola
00363199	Trumpet	00363204	Cello

Star Wars
16 songs
00350900	Flute	00350907	Horn
00350913	Oboe	00350908	Trombone
00350903	Clarinet	00350909	Violin
00350904	Alto Sax	00350910	Viola
00350905	Tenor Sax	00350911	Cello
00350906	Trumpet	00350914	Mallet

Taylor Swift
15 songs
00842532	Flute	00842537	Horn
00842533	Clarinet	00842538	Trombone
00842534	Alto Sax	00842539	Violin
00842535	Tenor Sax	00842540	Viola
00842536	Trumpet	00842541	Cello

Video Game Music
13 songs
00283877	Flute	00283883	Horn
00283878	Clarinet	00283884	Trombone
00283879	Alto Sax	00283885	Violin
00283880	Tenor Sax	00283886	Viola
00283882	Trumpet	00283887	Cello

Wicked
13 songs
00842236	Flute	00842241	Horn
00842237	Clarinet	00842242	Trombone
00842238	Alto Sax	00842243	Violin
00842239	Tenor Sax	00842244	Viola
00842240	Trumpet	00842245	Cello

HAL•LEONARD®

The Best-Selling Jazz Book of All Time Is Now Legal!

The Real Books are the most popular jazz books of all time. Since the 1970s, musicians have trusted these volumes to get them through every gig, night after night. The problem is that the books were illegally produced and distributed, without any regard to copyright law, or royalties paid to the composers who created these musical masterpieces.

Hal Leonard is very proud to present the first legitimate and legal editions of these books ever produced. You won't even notice the difference, other than all the notorious errors being fixed: the covers and typeface look the same, the song lists are nearly identical, and the price for our edition is even cheaper than the originals!

Every conscientious musician will appreciate that these books are now produced accurately and ethically, benefitting the songwriters that we owe for some of the greatest tunes of all time!

VOLUME 1

00240221	C Edition	$49.99
00240224	Bb Edition	$49.99
00240225	Eb Edition	$49.99
00240226	Bass Clef Edition	$49.99
00286389	F Edition	$39.99
00240292	C Edition 6 x 9	$39.99
00240339	Bb Edition 6 x 9	$44.99
00147792	Bass Clef Edition 6 x 9	$39.99
00200984	Online Backing Tracks: Selections	$45.00
00110604	Book/USB Flash Drive Backing Tracks Pack	$85.00
00110599	USB Flash Drive Only	$50.00

VOLUME 2

00240222	C Edition	$49.99
00240227	Bb Edition	$49.99
00240228	Eb Edition	$49.99
00240229	Bass Clef Edition	$49.99
00240293	C Edition 6 x 9	$39.99
00125900	Bb Edition 6 x 9	$39.99
00125900	The Real Book – Mini Edition	$39.99
00204126	Backing Tracks on USB Flash Drive	$55.00
00204131	C Edition – USB Flash Drive Pack	$85.00

VOLUME 3

00240233	C Edition	$49.99
00240284	Bb Edition	$49.99
00240285	Eb Edition	$49.99
00240286	Bass Clef Edition	$49.99
00240338	C Edition 6 x 9	$39.99

VOLUME 4

00240296	C Edition	$49.99
00103348	Bb Edition	$49.99
00103349	Eb Edition	$49.99
00103350	Bass Clef Edition	$49.99

VOLUME 5

00240349	C Edition	$49.99
00175278	Bb Edition	$49.99
00175279	Eb Edition	$49.99

VOLUME 6

00240534	C Edition	$49.99
00223637	Eb Edition	$49.99

Also available:

00154230	The Real Bebop Book C Edition	$34.99
00295069	The Real Bebop Book Eb Edition	$34.99
00295068	The Real Bebop Book Bb Edition	$34.99
00240264	The Real Blues Book	$39.99
00310910	The Real Bluegrass Book	$39.99
00240223	The Real Broadway Book	$39.99
00240440	The Trane Book	$25.00
00125426	The Real Country Book	$45.00
00269721	The Real Miles Davis Book C Edition	$29.99
00269723	The Real Miles Davis Book Bb Edition	$29.99
00240355	The Real Dixieland Book C Edition	$39.99
00294853	The Real Dixieland Book Eb Edition	$39.99
00122335	The Real Dixieland Book Bb Edition	$39.99
00240235	The Duke Ellington Real Book	$29.99
00240268	The Real Jazz Solos Book	$44.99
00240348	The Real Latin Book C Edition	$39.99
00127107	The Real Latin Book Bb Edition	$39.99
00120809	The Pat Metheny Real Book C Edition	$34.99
00252119	The Pat Metheny Real Book Bb Edition	$29.99
00240358	The Charlie Parker Real Book C Edition	$25.00
00275997	The Charlie Parker Real Book Eb Edition	$25.00
00118324	The Real Pop Book C Edition – Vol. 1	$45.00
00295066	The Real Pop Book Bb Edition – Vol. 1	$39.99
00286451	The Real Pop Book C Edition – Vol. 2	$45.00
00240331	The Bud Powell Real Book	$25.00
00240437	The Real R&B Book C Edition	$45.00
00276590	The Real R&B Book Bb Edition	$45.00
00240313	The Real Rock Book	$39.99
00240323	The Real Rock Book – Vol. 2	$39.99
00240359	The Real Tab Book	$39.99
00240317	The Real Worship Book	$35.00

THE REAL CHRISTMAS BOOK

00240306	C Edition	$39.99
00240345	Bb Edition	$35.00
00240346	Eb Edition	$35.00
00240347	Bass Clef Edition	$35.00

THE REAL VOCAL BOOK

00240230	Volume 1 High Voice	$40.00
00240307	Volume 1 Low Voice	$40.00
00240231	Volume 2 High Voice	$39.99
00240308	Volume 2 Low Voice	$39.99
00240391	Volume 3 High Voice	$39.99
00240392	Volume 3 Low Voice	$39.99
00118318	Volume 4 High Voice	$39.99
00118319	Volume 4 Low Voice	$39.99

Complete song lists online at www.halleonard.com

0223
318